HEALING THROUGH CARIN

A six week Bible based Study Course in Pastoral Care fo
lay people, suitable to be used during Lent or at any other

Howard Booth

Arthur James
BOOK PUBLISHERS

HEALING THROUGH CARING

First published in 1989
Reprinted 1991

British Library Cataloguing in Publication Data
Booth, Howard
Healing through caring.
1. Christian church. Pastoral work. Role of laity.
I. Title
265'.82

ISBN 0 85305 293 X

Made and printed in Great Britain by
The Guernsey Press Co. Ltd, Guernsey, Channel Islands.

Contents

Other books by Howard Booth

'On Parade!', Epworth Press, 1964
'Prayer Tools for Health and Healing', The Grail, 1978
'Stepping Stones to Christian Maturity', Bible Reading Fellowship, 1980
'In Search of Health and Wholeness' (Editor), Division of Social Responsibility, 1984
'Healing Experiences', Bible Reading Fellowship, 1985
'Healing IS Wholeness', Division of Social Responsibility & Churches' Council for Health & Healing, 1987
'Stepping Stones to Christian Maturity' second edition, Arthur James Limited, 1991

Booklets

'The Christian Nurse', McMillan, 1962
'Growing in Christian Confidence', Methodist Publishing House, 1986

Acknowledgements

The initial impetus to write these notes came from the Sturminster Newton Council of Christian Congregations. When we were planning our Lent Course for 1988 it was decided that we would try and help our people to think about effective pastoral care. I was asked to prepare the notes which appeared originally in duplicated form. Since then I have revised them and added suggestions for "A Topical Introduction" and for "A Closing Meditation".

I would like to dedicate "Healing Through Caring" to . . .

Arthur,
Mary,
Eric and
Sheila.

Four people who care . . .

Howard Booth

102a, Gawsworth Road,
Broken Cross,
Macclesfield, Cheshire.
SK11 8UE

HEALING THROUGH CARING

Introduction

Individuals are healed when they move forward into new experiences of healthier living. This may or may not include cure. Whatever be the means used to facilitate healing — medical, psychological, pastoral, or any other — they must always include care. Cures can sometimes be effected by purely mechanical means — drugs, surgery for instance — but people only find true healing when they know they are being cared for.

A certain Dr. Balint writing about general practice said that . . . "A Doctor's most important tool is himself (herself)". He stressed the importance of caring relationships which can help people in need to discover hope and begin to believe in themselves.

Caring often creates a more positive attitude towards life and can give meaning to living within limitations (see Paul's moving testimony in 2 Cor. 12:8-10), and indeed to dying. Whatever be the outcome, sincere caring is never wasted; in the divine economy it always pays dividends.

But Christian caring has an even deeper quality; it is really about loving. Many people are healed when they discover how both to give and receive love. Christian love is more profound than sentiment and more demanding than liking.

It is not difficult to love someone we like; it is very hard indeed to love someone we do not like. But many people's needs are expressed in just those ways which make them difficult to like. If no one ever shows love towards them their needs will remain unmet.

Today we have many different kinds of accredited helpers — doctors, lawyers, social workers, family therapists, priests, ministers, psychotherapists, counsellors — and many more. We would be hard-pressed without them. They are indispensable within society as it is today. Yet being an accredited helper does impose limitations on the relationship. It makes it uneven for one thing.

It is also possible for those with advanced professional training to become detached and clinical in their approach. This should not happen but, unhappily, it does *sometimes.* All the knowledge and expertise in the world will not adequately help people in need unless it is offered with caring compassion. "I may understand all knowledge and all secrets . . . but if I have no love . . ." (1 Cor. 13:2).

This Study Course seeks to emphasise the tremendous importance of the ordinary, day-by-day, caring relationships between individuals. These will not usurp professional expertise, nor contradict its insights. They may, however, provide just what is needed to complement what the professional carers may be offering; an additional listening ear, sympathy, understanding — and an entry into an awareness of God's love.

This latter never means applying religious pressure; it does mean that we see our caring relationships as set firmly within the dimension of the spiritual. This can provide the vital spark which might otherwise be missing and it can lead to a proper form of dependence — dependence on God. It may also mean that concerned and committed lay-persons may persevere in maintaining difficult relationships because they are being strengthened by the grace of God and guided by the Holy Spirit.

There is another reason why relationships between 'equals' can sometimes open areas of human experience which the 'professional and client' relationship may not touch. The very feeling of inability to help may lead to an admission of vulnerability which, when explored, can have healing consequences.

This course is then about the pastoral care which can be exercised by ordinary, committed lay people who are inspired by their Christian faith but who do not believe that there are simplistic religious answers to every problem. Such answers and solutions which are discovered will often come first through the medium rather than the message. Of course it is the message (the 'good news') which has inspired the medium and eventually the message becomes an essential part of the healing process. But God's love helps people to come alive when it is first expressed through human love and concern.

However, concerned and committed lay people do need to reflect upon their helping role and seek for insights which help them to love and care as helpfully and creatively as is possible. This course will therefore offer insights which arise from the experience and training of the professional carers, but it will not seek to add to their ranks. Hopefully it will provide them with the kind of support and assistance the best of them value so highly.

The Pattern of the Meetings

A brief suggested introduction to the particular aspect of caring which is being dealt with each week is first given. This introduction should be topical and lively. It is to open up the subject and to get the participants involved from the beginning. This can be achieved by a simple bit of home-made drama, a short role play, a modern parable or story, or a personal statement (testimony) from someone who has a genuine, relevant happening in their lives which they are prepared to share. The purpose of this is to raise issues and questions — not to supply answers.

The main substance of the evening lies in the group work for which every participant has prepared by working through the material supplied, including checking out and noting the various Bible references. The group work suggestions are based upon the premise that this work has been done *before* the meetings take place.

It is anticipated that the group work will give rise to suggestions for action. Indeed the way the discussion topics are introduced seeks to guarantee that challenges (corporate and individual) will arise. Such action is an essential feature of the course. There can be "no impression without expression" — as I recall from Sunday School teacher training courses I attended over 40 years ago. The principle still holds good in adult education.

The final stage of the meeting is the Meditation. A framework for this with suggestions is provided each week. However it is vital that the Meditation shall include the discoveries and resolutions made in the groups, so opportunity will need to be provided for these to be fed in by the participants themselves (perhaps through group leaders). Within the atmosphere of a quiet Meditation that which has been happening in the groups can reach down deeper into the minds and hearts of the course members. It is out of sincere resolves and a deepening spirituality that the course will be of real benefit to those who take part in it.

An Alternative

It is recognised that not all church groups will be willing to work in the way suggested so the main substance of the input material could be presented in the form of a series of addresses perhaps within Sunday worship, leading on to group activity either immediately on Church premises or later in the week in house groups. A group could then offer the fruits of one week's work within a Meditation on the following Sunday.

Some Pastoral Situations

(All the situations described below are a combination of fact and fiction. There is an element of truth in all of them and similar things have happened to real people. However they have been 'mixed' so as to avoid identification, and the details have been 'doctored' so as to provide a variety of different situations. They could be used to give ideas for the introductory Drama or Role Play or Story.)

Situation No. 1

My neighbour has just been round to tell me that her husband has died. It was quite sudden. A heart attack. He had been put into intensive care at the local hospital and had been there for just three days. I had taken her in twice to see him and he seemed to be making progress but she had been sent for urgently while I was out shopping. He died soon after she reached hospital and now she had come straight round to tell me. As soon as I answered the door I knew what had happened. The tears were streaming down her cheeks. "He's gone," she said. I put my arms around her and held her tight. My tears mingled with hers. She goes to her Church and I go to mine but while we have often discussed 'Church' matters, we have never said much to each other about our own personal faith. Now I felt that I ought to say something and I muttered a few words about his having 'gone home'. She didn't seem to like this: "But I want him here," she cried, "in our home. It's all so desperately unfair."

Situation No. 2

My colleague at the office has been looking more and more depressed and ill. He comes to work as in a dream. Today he managed to tell me the reason. His wife has left him. They have been married for 25 years and his two children are now both away from home — one married and one at University. She had told him two weeks ago that it was the children who had kept her at home although for her the marriage had been dead years ago. Now she had met someone who seemed to be offering her what she was looking for. He had not 'chased' her (so she said) but had been sympathetic and understanding. He was a widower and free to marry so she wanted a divorce. She was sorry but could not face the rest of her life tied within, what was for her, a dull and uninteresting relationship. My colleague was devastated. He had no suspicion that anything was wrong and was quite content with their rather pedestrian lifestyle. "What can I do?" he asked. My heart went out to him but I was at a complete loss to know what to say.

Situation No. 3

I am a widow and my son has just been arrested having been found in possession of drugs. My son! I brought him home from the Police Station and naturally asked him why? "I wanted to get a kick out of life," he answered. "A friend told me that this was the way to get what I wanted." My son! What can I do to help him?

Situation No. 4

Jim came to our Church when he moved into the area as a young General Practitioner working from the local Health Centre. Day by day he sees his patients and tries to help them. Most of them come with recognisable symptoms and he deals with them competently: medication, advice, referral to hospital. But quite a number of people who come to him do not seem to be ill in text-book ways. They are just not functioning properly. They worry about anything and everything. He shared the problem with us in general terms in our house group. Yes, there are certain psychotropic drugs he can prescribe and sometimes he does, but they only seem to help some for a time while other patients say that they can't cope without them. He doesn't like this, but to go on prescribing them seems to be the easiest way out. He has talked it over with his colleagues but they don't seem to be as concerned as he is. What shall he do?

Situation No. 5

One of my neighbours has no apparent problems. He is doing well at work; has a happy and supportive marriage and three healthy children. The other day he seemed in rather a strange mood when he was talking with me over the garden fence. "Do you ever wonder what life is all about?" he asked. "I do and I can't come up with an answer."

Situation No. 6

I met Claire who is a social worker when she came to talk to our Wives' Club about child abuse. We became friends and she pops round now and again for coffee and a chat. She talks about her work in general terms but never divulges any personal details about her clients. The other day she told me that she had started to go to various Retreat Houses just occasionally at week-ends. She felt that she needed to find things out about herself and had met people there who were engaged in a similar search. She also shared with me recently that she feels that she is being drawn to re-discover her lost Christian faith. However she accompanied this by saying that she didn't think that this required her to become religious and attend Church. My response to this seemed to be trite and inadequate.

Situation No. 7

My husband had to pay a visit to our solicitor about a legal contract. They both belong to the local cricket team and so know one another fairly well. He didn't seem to be busy and wanted to talk about his attitudes towards the varied problems he faces day by day: marital breakdown; family difficulties; neighbour pressures; custody orders for children; the odd criminal case. He is a good lawyer, widely respected and he didn't break any confidences. He told my husband that he often felt inadequate to deal with the emotional consequences of legal action. He finds himself getting upset and feels deeply for some of his clients. He doesn't go to Church but the other day, to his own surprise, he found himself asking a client if he had thought of going to see the Parish Vicar. The response had been blank amazement!

Situation No. 8

I discovered something the other day which, up to now, I haven't shared with anybody. A cousin of mine works in the admissions office of a hospital about 40 miles away. She told me over the telephone that the minister from our church is attending there for psychotherapy. He has an anxiety problem and his G.P. had referred him to this hospital so that he would be less likely to meet up with any of his own people. The referral letter said that this was at his own request. I upset my cousin by telling her that she had no right to tell me. The details about our minister were confidential information which she should have kept to herself. But I feel uneasy about it all. Why couldn't he share his needs with some of us? Why try to keep up appearances in this way? I happen to know that he has been a kind and understanding pastor to many people in their needs. Also he often urges us all to recognise that our Church is a healing community. If he had told us something of his own needs, couldn't we, in some way, have helped him? Who cares for the carers?

Topical Introduction

Three different people each re-tell a gospel incident illustrating how Jesus cared for people. An interesting way of doing this is by the imaginative use of the first person, the storyteller taking the part of the person who has experienced the caring love of Jesus. There is abundant material for this kind of exercise in Alan Dale's *New World* (Oxford University Press). Here is an example based on Mark 5:25-34 but see also page 15 in *New World*.

I had been ill for 12 years and the doctors could do nothing for me. Mine was a distressing complaint — continuous bleeding — which made me a social outcast. I had heard people talking about this Jesus and the ways in which he helped sick people and slowly the conviction had dawned on me that, if only I could get near enough to him, he could help me.

The crowd around Jesus made it very difficult but I was determined to succeed. When I got within range of him, however, my courage failed and I dared not speak. The only thing I could do was to grasp his outer garment momentarily, but even that made me feel better.

Then I heard his voice asking a question: "Who touched me?" One of his disciples pointed out the throng around him and suggested that it was impossible to know. But Jesus was not satisfied. He looked around with his deep, piercing, but kindly eyes and said: "This person touched me in a special way. Who was it?"

Trembling I fell down before him and told him everything. His reply chased away my fear and filled my heart with joy: "Daughter," he said, "your trust in me has made you better; go home and don't worry any more."

I did just as he said — but with a truly thankful heart.

Another suitable incident is that of "The Blind Man" (Mark 8:22-26) but see also page 16 in *New World*. See also Mark 6:31-46 "The Desert Meal" page 21 in *New World*.

Material for Study and Reflection

Preachers on ascending into a new pulpit sometimes find a card on the desk before them which says: "Sir, we would see Jesus". This is our purpose in this first study — to see Jesus and to reflect upon the many different ways in which he cared for people.

It is truly remarkable that the records of the life of Jesus and the stories he told, together with his conversations and pithy sayings, are still inspiring and stimulating the hearts and minds of so many people living two thousand years afterwards. This is even more remarkable when you consider the different culture patterns of his day and ours. He lived among farmers and fishermen and many of his stories reflect this background. To his Jewish forbears religion was an essential part of their whole lives; there was for instance no division between religion and politics. We live in a more sophisticated society in which the combination of religion and politics tends to spark off controversy.

We also 'see Jesus' through centuries of Church history which has seen many dark and sombre pages in which the sins of the followers of Jesus have tended to cloud the picture. It is not always easy to get close to the life and teaching of Jesus because of the schisms and mistakes which are very much part of our institutional Christianity.

But again and again the miracle does happen. Through our reading of the New Testament and our reflections upon its teachings, Christ comes alive! This is the clear intention of this course of study. We are going to do our own bit of 'demythologising'. We are going to try to clear away the misunderstandings and misconceptions which come partly from our different culture and partly from our Church 'conditioning'. As we endeavour to take a fresh look at Jesus perhaps we can pray . . . *"Lord Jesus, show me your real self and help me to discover afresh how you cared for people and how important your example of caring could be to me."*

1. Jesus accepted people just as they were

The disciples were a motley crew. They were ambitious (Luke 9:46), selfish and power-seeking (Luke 22:24-27), lacking in real understanding (Mark 10:35-40). Yet Jesus accepted them, believed in them, trusted them, forgave them when they betrayed him and let him down (John 21:15-19). Slowly they discerned just who he was and what was his purpose. Eventually they became the ones to whom he entrusted the continuance of his work (Matthew 28:16-20). Jesus had succeeded in making "a silk purse out of a sow's ear".

Certain groups of people were despised by the orthodox, religious people of the days when Jesus lived: tax-collectors who connived with the Roman oppressors (Matthew 9:10-13); prostitutes (John 8:1-11), and lepers (Luke 17:11-19). Jesus accepted them. He did not approve of tax collectors who cheated; nor of women who sold their bodies. Those who suffered from leprosy were not necessarily sinners although the popular belief of his day was that sickness was the consequence of sin. Jesus accepted them; forgave them where this was necessary, healed them and invited them to participate in the Kingdom which had been inaugurated by his coming (Luke 4:16-21).

Jesus then cared for people and helped them to move forward into new experiences of healthier living. This task is now ours. While Jesus very much wanted those he helped to become a conscious part of the Kingdom, through their penitence and faith, he does not seem to have made this a condition of his helping them. The man at the Pool of Bethsaida was healed by Jesus *before* he spoke to him about his sins. (Compare John 5:8 with John 5:14 noting the word 'afterwards').

The clear implication of this example for us is that we are invited to care for people whatever their attitude is towards our Church or even towards Jesus. The very fact of our caring is a sign that the Kingdom is active in our midst, but we continue to care even though there is no obvious response in commitment to Christ. Which groups in society today are conscious of being rejected? Those who suffer from Aids? Those who have come from other countries to live among us and who are of a different colour and culture? The disabled who desire even more than ramps and wide toilet doors in public buildings, to feel that they belong and are accepted as human beings in their own right?

These groups constitute a challenge to our caring ministry but there are also many individuals known to us who desperately need to be accepted and loved.

2. Jesus opened up people's minds and made them think

This is a clear pointer to a significant way in which

Jesus cared for people. As an educator and pioneer in leadership development Jesus was light years ahead of his time. By putting the gospel truths in story form (parables) Jesus was inviting people to think for themselves. He enshrined profound principles in word pictures and then invited his hearers to make their own response. He does not seem to have applied unhealthy pressure upon people to conform. He loved them and gave himself for them. When they followed him in love and loyalty, he rejoiced. This was the ultimate blessing; this was the reason why the Father had sent him into the world (Luke 15: 7, 10 and 32).

James Stewart in his splendid teaching manual on *The Life and Teaching of Jesus Christ* (Church of Scotland Publications) made this point clear: "As you turn the pages of the gospels, one fact stares out at you; the quite amazing patience of Jesus with the men he had to teach, his steadfast refusal to dictate to them or compel them or bend them to his will, his overwhelming respect for their personalities."

How different this is to the way in which some of the sects operate! The Scientologists and Moonies seem to practice psychological techniques familiar to those who have lived under totalitarian regimes. They brainwash people into being their followers. But this is a different process from making disciples.

Christian disciples are made when individuals realise that, as Jesus clearly taught, God loves them and invites their full and free response. This kind of caring takes risks. People can reject as well as accept. But it is only this possibility which makes for mature and responsible decisions. To go back to Alan Dale again, this time in the Preface to *New World*: "Jesus did not want 'Yes-men'; he wanted people to 'judge of themselves', to know what they believe and to love what they know. Only so can he become for us either Leader or Lord."

3. Jesus linked care with Prayer

Take a typical day in the life of Jesus as described by Mark (Mark 1: 21-39). It began at 10 a.m. in the Synagogue where he taught *with authority*; but not the authority of the 'big shout'; not the authority of the demagogue — but rather the authority of his own authenticity. He then experienced conflict with the Pharisees because he calmed down a mentally deranged man. Then he brought healing to Simon's mother-in-law and this resulted in many other needy people coming to him for help. The whole process was tiring in the extreme. The exhaustion he felt could not be made good by sleep alone. Early the following morning he was praying to his Father on the lonely mountainside. The renewing of body, mind and spirit which came from his times of prayer were an essential aspect of the life-style Jesus chose for himself. Prayer was inseparable from care. It was through his relationship with his Father that he was able to sustain the heavy loads placed upon him.

When the greatest test of all came to Jesus (Luke 22:39-54) he went, with his friends to Olive Hill. There he agonised over what lay ahead, knowing that he could only survive the ordeal if he was given strength from outside himself. The only way to open up the channels to make this possible was through prayer. So Jesus prayed with all his heart.

His friends, who had also been under strain, could not stand the pace. They slept. But Jesus knew that they also would have to struggle in prayer if they were going to make the grade and be useful to him (v.46).

A recent book on counselling has a chapter entitled *The Untapped Resource of Counselling — Prayer.* (See *Self-Talk, Imagery and Prayer in Counselling* by H. Norman Wright, Word Books, Milton Keynes). Prayer is not just an insertion of religion into the counselling process; it is a recognition that our deepest needs can only ultimately be met by divine resources. Jesus told his disciples, and through them he tells us, to ask, to seek and to knock (Matthew 7:7). This does not mean that, as those who are trying to help others, all we have to do is to put the troublesome issue before God, and expect to get an immediate answer. It does mean however, that we discover a greater sensitivity in our dealing with people in need; it does mean a deepening in the relationship between us, and it does mean that from time to time flashes of insight come to both parties which would not have come if we had not prayed. Paul reminds us that we can even call upon the Holy Spirit to guide our prayers (Romans 8:26-27).

Fear of the future, fear of death, fear of loneliness; these are at the centre of many emotional problems. Through the use of prayer we can often replace negative, destructive thoughts with wholesome, creative concepts and ideas. By this means long standing habit patterns can be replaced by 'the fruits of the Spirit' (see Galatians 5:22-26).

Suggestions for Group Activity

1. Take the following Sayings of Jesus as translated by Alan Dale in *New World* and discuss what you think each saying means for Christians today. If it seems right to your group, compose a sentence prayer relating to each saying to feed in to the Meditation.

   a) God is your Father and you must live in his way. He cares for everybody — bad people and good people, honest people and dishonest people. See how the sun shines and the rain falls on all their farms alike.

   b) If you want to help me you must give all your heart to it. You must be ready to let people do their worst to you. And you must keep your eyes on me.

   c) When you listen, you must really listen.

2. The first disciples have been described as the 'apprentices' of Jesus. Think of some of the details associated with being an apprentice:

   a) An initial contract.

   b) Beginning by doing menial tasks.

   c) Watching the skilled person at work.

   d) Being allowed to perform simple tasks.

   e) Making mistakes and being corrected.

   f) Being entrusted with more important tasks.

   g) Qualifying and being authorised to act.

   Recall events in the relationships between Jesus and his disciples which illustrate any of those stages. Then ask if there are any insights to be discovered which give impetus to your own caring ministry.

(**Author's Note:** Through reading Alan Dale's *New World* when it was first published in 1967, Jesus came alive for me in a new and gripping way.)

Suggestions for a Closing Meditation

"Christianity had at its heart a person and a life before it had a creed and a code; and the thing that is characteristic of the great documents of the New Testament is their passionate devotion to the person and their spontaneous reproduction of the life . . . The New Testament has not attained to the dignity of a creed and a code; it has what is much better — a passionate love of Christ and a living fellowship of the brethren."

(T. W. Manson, *On Paul and John,* quoted in the Preface to *New World,* OUP)

Jesus said . . . I am the WAY, the TRUTH and the LIFE. Allow your imagination to be inspired by each of these words in turn.

THE WAY

Visualise a narrow path winding up the mountainside. Although narrow, it is clear and distinct but some of the signposts have been tampered with and are pointing in the wrong direction. Ask for guidance to know the right way to go.

THE TRUTH

"What is truth?" Pilate asked Jesus. Yet the embodiment of truth stood immediately before him. We cannot possess complete and correct knowledge about everything and everybody, but we need a vital clue so that we can make sense of life. Jesus is that vital clue. In the silence invite him to give an even greater meaning and signficance to your life.

THE LIFE

"I am come that you might have life and have it more abundantly," said Jesus. In the New Testament and particularly in the writings of John this 'life' is a divine energy; the essence of being — which transforms and renews. Ask him directly for a new influx of this gift of life.

PROVIDE OPPORTUNITIES FOR EACH GROUP TO FEED IN THEIR SENTENCE PRAYERS RELATING TO THE SAYINGS OF JESUS.

CLOSE WITH AN ACT OF DEDICATION WHICH COULD INCLUDE A HYMN OF THANKSGIVING FOR THE BIBLE.

THE LAST WORD: "I have lived among you as a waiter who looks after the needs of other people" (A word from Jesus as translated by Alan Dale in *New World* page 126).

Topical Introduction

A Role Play

The situation to be depicted is that the Minister/Vicar of St. Stephen's Church is off duty with what seems to be a nervous illness. The Church Wardens/Stewards/Deacons have met to discuss what — if anything — can be done to help him. In the role play the following points (among others) are made:

1. The Minister/Vicar is totally dedicated to his Church work at every level — locally; in the wider area and even nationally.
2. He refuses all offers of administrative help — paid or voluntary.
3. It is known that his doctor considers him unsuitable for the office he holds. (This has emerged from the minister himself not from the doctor).
4. The minister's wife also feels that he may be in the wrong calling but knows that any suggestion of a change would just pile on the guilt.
5. The Bishop/Chairman/Moderator is willing to move him to a lighter job, but when this was suggested the minister begged not to be moved as this would be seen as failure.

The discussion includes the participants talking about how they each try to maintain their own health. Eventually they decide to send two of their number to see him and they work out together what they will try to say.

Alternative

Two people have investigated stress related illnesses and speak briefly about their causes and recognisable symptoms.

(Two books which would help are *Ministry Burnout* by John Sanford published by Arthur James and *Holistic Living* by Patrick Pietroni, published by Dent).

NB: In appropriate cases the minister could just as easily be a lady, in which case suitable adjustments would need to be made in the discussion. This note relates to the Role Play.

Material for Study and Reflection

"Look after number one" is a well-known saying — but it is a recipe for disaster. Yet many live by this philosophy — sometimes quite unconsciously. People who are grasping, acquisitive, lacking proper concern for the welfare of others; such people are sowing the seeds of discontent and ultimate frustration. When they finally come to appreciate their true condition they realise that they are rich in possessions, but poverty stricken in those essential deep and abiding relationships which make life worthwhile and meaningful.

At the other end of the scale there are those who totally exhaust themselves serving others. They are involved in every kind of public service. Sometimes their own loved ones and family suffer from this total dedication. Marriages find it hard to survive and children grow up bereft of the close awareness of parental love from either father or mother, which their proper development as persons desperately needs.

Yet another type of person constantly denigrates themselves. Whatever they do by way of public or church service others could do it far better. When they are pressed into accepting certain responsibilities they demur on account of their lack of talent and ability. They are often difficult people to deal with.

Over against all these is the true Christian estimate of the value of every individual personality. There is a proper love of self made quite explicit by Jesus in the second of the great commandments: "Thou shalt love thy neighbour *as thyself*" (Mark 12:31 and see also Romans 13:9). If the basic aim of good pastoral care is to help people to realise that they are loved and can themselves be loving, it is quite apparent that this must begin in our loving and appreciating ourselves. Many things flow from this but good habits are based upon sound Christian principles. If we get our understanding of God wrong we shall make many consequent mistakes. So we begin with God!

1. God loves me

The whole thrust of the Bible is to reveal an outgoing God whose prime motivation is to share his love with the people he has brought into being. In the Old Testament it is made clear that God loves the nation, Israel (See Deuteronomy 7:7-8; Hosea 11:1 and 4). The prophet Jeremiah helps us to see that

God's love is also directed towards individuals (see Jeremiah 31:3). The New Testament shows that God's love is for every human person (see Romans 5:8 and I John 4:9-10).

But God's love is not sentimental; it is always for our ultimate good and sometimes, this seems hard. There is discipline in love (see Hebrews 12:6).

2. God understands me

A book by a Roman Catholic priest and theologian, Father Simon Tugwell, O.P. is entitled *Ways of Imperfection* (Darton, Longman and Todd). It is a masterly survey of spirituality across the centuries with thumb nail sketches of many of the masters of the inner life.

As the title of the book implies, we are *imperfect* people. We have not yet attained to our goal. The mark of a true disciple is persevering determination (see Philippians 3:13-14). We have not yet aspired to perfection but God understands us. He knows that we are frail, but he has made certain promises which he will always keep (see 2 Corinthians 12:9 and Colossians 1:13). Therefore we should not be discouraged; we are followers of The Way and this implies that we are travellers who are en route but who have not yet arrived. Nevertheless we are travelling hopefully (see John 14:4-6). That Way is Christ's Way and along it there are opportunities for penitence, forgiveness and many new beginnings. God accepts me just as I am (as we saw in Week 1), and thus we are able to move on to higher ground. No one is ever good enough for the service of our Lord Jesus Christ. God is well satisfied with Wayfarers who are serious and in earnest; he makes full allowance for our human weakness (see Psalm 103:14).

3. God is available to me

There are a number of ways in which we can make the most of God's availability:

a) Through prayer, contemplation and meditation. God is to be found in the silence but silence can be void and empty. We help to create the conditions for God to get through to us by setting aside time to cultivate his presence. We can begin with simple relaxation exercises then move on to discover inner quiet by slowly repeating a verse from scripture such as "Be still and know that I am God" (Psalm 46:10). Surveying a beautiful picture or sculpture can also help us to discover our own *inner room*. Mother Mary Clare suggests that . . . "the normal development of prayer takes root in the context of silence and listening . . ." (*Encountering the Depths,* Darton, Longman and Todd).

b) Through worship and the sacraments. When we lift up our hearts to God in this way we are purified and made more whole. The solitary journey needs to be complemented by the corporate endeavour. What we discern in the silence will sometimes be corrected and re-directed when we meet with others to rejoice and celebrate.

4. God renews me

Christopher Bryant has explored the teaching of C. G. Jung and related some of his insights to the Christian pilgrimage. He suggests that . . . "to become aware of God the individual must enter into the darkness with him; the unexplored hinterland of the personality. The old masters insist that the experience of God is no mere intellectual knowledge; it is heart knowledge . . ." (*Jung and the Christian Faith,* Darton, Longman and Todd).

Our renewal as persons depends upon our accepting the shadow side of our personality; coming to terms with it — and even loving it. The journey towards God involves us in discovering dark corners and unlit recesses. Then comes cleansing and illumination and the way ahead becomes clearer and more distinct (see 1 Samuel 16:7; Proverbs 4:23; Jeremiah 17:9 and 2 Corinthians 4:6).

Only hearts that are truly open to God will be renewed by him. This inner experience of renewal is vital in our caring for others. It will come across in the mutual recognition of those things which are vital for growth. This is dealt with in greater length in Study No. 4 but potential growth is vitally linked with a proper appreciation of self. One of the interesting things happening today is that this experience of inward renewal is coming via charismatic channels and also among those whose search for God is along the lines of contemplative spirituality.

5. God equips me

In our genuine desire to be able to help more people through pastoral care, we shall naturally feel a need to be better equipped. Indeed this is the purpose of this course. But while there are certain things we can discover by listening, reading, sharing in discussion, looking at case studies etc., at this stage we are seeking to recognise that our essential equipment comes directly from God. One element in the total package will certainly be an increased awareness and sensitivity. Individuals will often open up a pastoral relationship by revealing only the *outer garments* of their true situation. As we are more and more open to God we shall be given the gift of discernment (see 1 Corinthians 2:4 and 1 Corinthians 12:10).

Of course the greatest gift of all that God imparts is the gift of love (see 1 Corinthians 13). It is the ability to love the unlovable and to persevere with what seems impossible, which is God's greatest gift to us. When you begin to feel the wisdom of God breaking through into your heart and mind and bringing light to the pastoral issue you are struggling with, then you will have a growing confidence in your ability to help others because you will be increasingly aware that God is helping you (see Hebrews 4:12).

6. The practical consequences

When we have that inner assurance that our understanding of the nature of God is valid and right, there are certain practical implications which follow, all of which relate to the proper appreciation of our selves. They relate to . . .

a) Our bodies. These are described as 'members of Christ' (1 Corinthians 6:15) and 'temples of the Holy Spirit' (1 Corinthians 6:19). Care of our physical beings through proper diet, regular exercise, times of rest and recreation, these are not optional extras but absolute necessities.

b) Our minds. 'A sound mind' (2 Tim. 1:7) is not a closed mind (2 Corinthians 3:14) but open to new thoughts and new ideas (see Romans 12:2). We need at times to be disturbed and not just to read and listen to those who make us comfortable.

c) Our spirits — our inner beings. This is what most of this study has been about but for a combination of all three see 1 Thessalonians 5:23.

Suggestions for Group Activity

1. How do the following ideas based on Biblical verses help to shape your understanding of a meaningful Christian life?

   a) Followers of Christ must deny themselves, take up their own cross and then follow him (Luke 9:23).

   b) The body should be kept under subjection (1 Corinthians 9:27).

   c) His yoke is easy and his burden light (Matthew 11:30).

   d) He offers rest to those who labour and are heavy laden (Matthew 11:28).

   e) Renewal and restoration is for those who wait on the Lord (Isaiah 40:31).

   Consider if, as a group you could offer a contribution to the Meditation saying something like . . . "Lord we have come to see that our Christian lives must be made up of . . . a) . . . . b) . . . c) . . . d) etc. We ask for your help to live up to what we believe."

2. You are writing an article on "The Christian Response to Stress". Decide what points must be included in the article. Perhaps one of the group could then undertake to write the points up in article form and submit it for inclusion in the Church Magazine or Newsletter.

(See book references in The Topical Introduction.)

Suggestions for a Closing Meditation

"Be still and know that I am God" (Psalm 46:10).

BE STILL

"You are precious in my sight and honoured, and I love you" (Isaiah 43:4).

"We love because he first loved us" (1 John 4:19).

At the centre of the world there is a 'still point' which is God himself.

AND KNOW

"This is life eternal, that they may know thee, the only true God, and Jesus Christ whom thou hast sent" (John 17:3).

"Grow in grace and in the knowledge of our Lord and Saviour Jesus Christ" (2 Peter 3:18).

"At the deepest part of us there is that which can only be itself when it lets go beyond itself. So, in relation to God, we become ourselves. He does not destroy what he has made but gently enables it to be itself. The union of our spirit with his, or rather his with ours, is life itself . . ." (Brother Bernard in *Open to God* — Fount Original).

THAT I AM GOD

"I am the Lord, I change not" (Malachi 3:6).

"He gives new life to those who are worn out; he revives those who are ready to drop! Commandoes get tired and faint, seasoned veterans fall out with fatigue; but those who trust God grow stronger and stronger — soaring like eagles, running without tiring, marching without flagging" (Isaiah 40:29-31 as translated by Alan Dale in *Winding Quest* — OUP).

"The pulse of the world is the heartbeat of God, and the dynamic presence of the living God is immanent in his creation. In him we live, move and have our being; from him we come and to him we go . . ." (Brother Ramon in *Life's Changing Seasons,* Marshall Pickering).

THE GROUPS OFFER THEIR PRAYERS

Sing "Be still and know that I am God" as a Chorus.

THE LAST WORD

Speak, Lord, in the stillness,
While we wait on thee,
Hush our hearts to listen —
in expectancy.

Topical Introduction

What follows really did happen.

A certain Church had a large, modern Health Centre built immediately next door. At the time that the Health Centre was officially opened the minister put a large poster on his Church Notice Board with the following declaration printed in bold letters:

THIS CHURCH IS ALSO A HEALTH CENTRE

Following this, several people wrote letters to the newspaper asking for clarification and the minister was invited to answer questions on local radio and appear on regional TV. The debate centred around two questions —

HOW CAN A CHURCH BE DESCRIBED AS A HEALTH CENTRE?

WAS THE NEW HEALTH CENTRE REALLY A HEALTH CENTRE AT ALL SINCE ITS MAIN ACTIVITIES WERE TO TREAT SICK PEOPLE?

Another development was that a local Natural Health Group asked if they could hold meetings in the new Health Centre and permission was refused. This gave rise to further local controversy and more letters to the local newspaper.

In this topical introduction use could be made of the above events and three people could be invited to speak for two minutes each on . . . . . .

1. My Church is a health centre because . . .
2. The Medical and Social Services should put more emphasis on prevention because . . .
3. There should be greater co-operation between the NHS and the voluntary agencies which exist to promote good health because . . .

Alternative

Persuade a group of health professionals — doctors, nurses, health visitors, mid-wives, etc. to arrange the 20 minute introduction on the theme, PREVENTION IS BETTER THAN CURE.

Material for Study and Reflection

Preventive health care is, at last, gaining a higher place on the public's agenda. From an economic point of view governments are realising that better health education to prevent the onset of illness and disease is, in the long run, less costly than expensive cures. Surprisingly, only a minority of health professionals seem keen to become involved. Perhaps this is because their training has been directed towards cure rather than prevention, and also because there is more glamour in curative medicine and greater satisfaction in seeing sick people get better. However "it is an ill wind . . . ." and shortage of resources in the curative sector is causing those in authority to look much more carefully at preventive health care. The dangers of tobacco smoking and the excessive use of alcohol are being pointed out in a variety of ways, as is the positive value of a healthy diet, regular exercise and a sensible rhythm of life with time for work, relaxation and leisure.

In a similar way we often associate caring with responding to a crisis: an illness; an accident; a bereavement; a family separation; the loss of a job. These all give rise to situations which obviously need caring and understanding support. But, as with preventive medicine, is there caring which can go on outside of crisis situations? If so, how do we get involved in preventive caring?

1. By realising the importance of ordinary relationships

We know that the way babies and children are cared for in their earliest years contributes towards their eventual ability to deal with crisis situations when they have to face them. If they are loved sensibly within a stable home environment, and if that love includes wise discipline, then they are likely to develop naturally towards growing maturity. On the other hand if they are 'spoiled' or submitted to a persistently harsh and punitive regime, they are likely to grow into inadequate adults who will find the normal strains and stresses of life too much for them.

In a similar manner our day-to-day, ordinary relationships provide opportunities for preventive caring. There are many normal situations which can so easily deteriorate into crises by unwise handling, a lack of sympathetic understanding, and an inability to control ourselves.

So thought should be given to them, their significance and importance assessed and, especially when things go wrong, time spent in reflection upon the mistakes made.

So, in any one day —

a) Have I encouraged the people I have met and so helped them to feel stronger and be more purposeful (see Acts 28:15)?

b) Have I shared something I possess with another human being (see Acts 4:32-37)? [This need not necessarily be a material item.]

c) Have I provided space for someone who needed to talk (see John 21:15-17)? [Do you think that there might have been silences in this conversation?]

d) Have I had the grace to apologise for an act or word I later felt unhappy about (see Luke 15:18)?

2. By contributing towards a helpful fellowship group

Groups abound for all kinds of purposes. Some are task oriented, members coming together in pursuit of a common task like the threat of an airport or nuclear power station being built in the vicinity. Others are idea centred. They are arranged for those who want to meet together to share information and thoughts about specialised subjects. Some of our Church groups are like this. The groups we are mainly concerned about in this course however, are *person centred* groups. Such groups may centre around the Bible or being prepared for confirmation. House groups can be both *idea* and *person centred*. However we are thinking about groups which help people to grow and develop, groups where it is possible to express feelings and build each other up. Through belonging to such groups people can be strengthened and enabled, so that when crises do come they are ready and prepared, and they have the support system they need well established.

Features of such groups are —

a) Facilitating leadership which encourages open communication between all members of the group (see 2 Timothy 1: 13-14).

b) No domination by the leader or any other member of the group (see John 10:3 note *leading* but not *driving*).

c) The acceptance of silence as a positive

feature both during times of sharing and in group prayer. When our voices are silent then God's voice may be heard (see Psalm 46:10 and 1 Thessalonians 4:11).

d) The creation of an atmosphere in which feelings can be expressed and fear and anxiety exposed (see 1 John 3: 19-24).

3. By developing a greater sense of involvement in worship

Worship is the principal activity for which the Church exists. This always includes opportunity for individuals to voice their personal thanksgiving; to express their sorrow for failure — and to be assured of God's gracious forgiveness.

For some the worship of their local Church is too formal and unchanging; for others worship has become too 'folksy' and informal. Some are happy when God is addressed in direct, personal terms; others feel that this detracts from the sense of mystery and awe they feel is necessary for their own uplift and satisfaction.

Many churches try to make provision for a variety of 'tastes' within the pattern of their worship services, but in this exercise let us think not so much of 'tastes' as of people's deepest needs being met.

a) How can we make sure that praise is personal as well as corporate (see 1 Peter 2:5)?

b) Are there means whereby we can enable the formal acts of confession and the declaration of forgiveness to come alive in vivid and personal ways (see 1 John 1: 8-9)?

c) How can we develop a true sense of togetherness in worship which enables people to *feel* that they belong to the Family of God and are citizens in his Kingdom (see Ephesians 3: 14-19)?

4. By promoting educational programmes which help to avoid destructive stress

It is a sad but true fact that Christian workers, ministers, priests and those who serve as volunteers in Church related projects, often suffer from stress and sometimes from breakdown. This may have its root in childhood experiences but it may also be due to a misunderstanding of the gospel message. Throughout Christian history it has always been easy for Christians to slip into the error of legalism. The

Christian Faith is seen as setting high and unattainable standards, and consequent failure brings frustration amd sometimes desperation. This was of course Paul's experience (see Romans 7:14ff). The consequences of unresolved struggles are always continuing stressful experiences. The battle is constantly fought but never won. The longer the struggle goes on the more devastating become its debilitating effects.

Such programmes should —

a) Provide counsellors who are trained to communicate the truth about the gospel offer as being about latching into a source of power which enables us to be, not so much paragons of virtue, as humble disciples of Jesus Christ. It is he who will deliver us and enable us (see 2 Peter 1: 3-4). The gospel message is not about impossible goals but adequate resources (see 1 Corinthians 10:13).

b) Utilise our mutual vulnerability. Those who are able to acknowledge their own incompleteness (see Romans 12:3) are often able to help one another. Wounded people *can* help each other (see Proverbs 27:6; Isaiah 53:5).

c) Recognise that good spiritual directors can facilitate good preventive care but realise, at the same time, that we can be helpful guides to one another (see Romans 15:7).

An American, Dr. Howard Clinebell, has some helpful things to say about a Church's preventive caring ministry. He suggests that the church's message can be "A constructive, creative, healing, life-affirming force and a rich source of courage, strength and growth for many people". He rightly insists that "A local church works best for mental health when it is true to its mission as a church and not when it attempts to become a mental health agency . . . Its rich contribution to mental health comes because it has vitality and supernatural power." *(Mental Health through Christian Community,* Abingdon Press, USA).

Suggestions for Group Activity

1. After each of the four sections in this week's study there are questions asked or points made each with Biblical references. Take each of the questions and points made in turn and go round the group for one comment on each, including some mention of the Bible material. Do not, at this stage, stop to discuss any point — simply get an individual comment. This should get everyone involved.

2. Here is a list of projects which have actually taken place in various churches all of which could be said to have preventive implications.

    a) A training course about ageing and retirement (very popular).

    b) A training course about parenting (not so popular).

    c) Relaxation and Meditation Groups.

    d) A regular series of leisure days.

    e) A 'University of Life' series in which well qualified lecturers spoke about all aspects of health and social competence (very popular).

    f) A Council of Churches invited all local doctors and clergy to meet to talk over matters of mutual interest.

    g) A group of churches approached the Social Services Department and asked if premises and personnel (voluntary) could be utilised to meet any social needs in the community.

Are any of the above projects worth thinking about and perhaps adapting in your local situation? Feed any possibilities into the Meditation and ask God for guidance.

Suggestions for a Closing Meditation

"Every human being has a great, yet often unknown, gift to care, to be compassionate; to become present to the other; to listen, to hear and to receive. If that gift could be set free and made available, miracles could take place."
(Henri J. M. Nouwen in *Out of Solitude,* Ave Maria Press)

Against a very soft musical background repeat slowly some of the key verses from Romans 12 as translated by Alan Dale in *New World* (OUP).

> "Don't try to do what everybody does; let God keep your mind alive and ready to think new thoughts and you'll be a very different person to what you were."

> "Don't go about with high and mighty ideas about your own importance. Think sensibly about yourselves, in the light of what your trust in God has already told you about God's love."

> "Be a real family, warm-hearted in your care for one another."

> "In hard times stand your ground, never forget to pray."

> "Share other people's happiness and other people's sadness."

INVITE THE GROUPS TO PRESENT THEIR IDEAS ABOUT POSSIBLE PREVENTIVE PROJECTS AND PRAY FOR GUIDANCE.

THE LAST WORD — "Everybody has heard the old adage that an ounce of prevention is worth a pound of cure. This is well established in medicine and a little reflection would suggest that prevention is at the core of much biblical teaching. By giving information, speaking to needs, proclaiming divine truth, and encouraging believers to pray for one another — this encourages both psychological and spiritual growth." (From *Innovative Approaches to Counselling,* Gary Collins, Word Books).

Topical Introduction

Jim was facing a crisis. He had just been told that he had the first signs of Multiple Sclerosis (MS). He had his own business which was, he believed, entirely dependent upon himself. His wife was shattered, but being a reasonably strong person she was determined to help him in every possible way. But she was unsure how Jim would react to his illness.

> *JIM 1: "I'm finished. I may live for a few years but I shall get steadily worse. There's no future for me. I'll sell the business and hope to have enough to live on till I die. Then what will happen to my wife, God only knows!"*

Jim deteriorated quickly, mentally and physically. He developed an enormous 'chip on his shoulder'; grumbled incessantly and made enormous demands on his wife which drove her to distraction. In the end she had a breakdown and Jim went into hospital where he died. Few people were sorry.

> *JIM 2: "I'm finished but I won't lie down quietly. I'll carry on with the business and make as much money as I can. Then I'll go into a private Nursing Home. I'm not going to be a burden on my wife. I know she'll want to look after me but I'm not going to let her. Sometimes you have to be cruel to be kind. She can have a divorce and marry a real man."*

Jim's wife was completely taken aback by his attitude. She pleaded with him to let her help him in the business and in the home. But he was adamant. His own plan worked and he eventually went into a private Nursing Home getting a warped satisfaction out of being a martyr. His wife felt rejected and useless. Eventually she did divorce him and remarry, but for the rest of her life she lived with feelings of rejection and guilt. Jim lived for ten years after his initial diagnosis.

> *JIM 3: "I'm not going to let MS beat me. I may have a long remission and be able to carry on working*

for years and years. I'll take my best workman into the business and make him a partner. My wife will come in as well and together we'll make something out of life. I'll do everything possible to provide for her in the future, but its the present I'm interested in now. I'll also get alongside others with the same illness and learn from them."

Jim lived a meaningful life for twenty years after the onset of his illness. He helped many other MS sufferers by his attitude towards his illness. His wife said that those twenty years were precious and full of meaning.

Material for Study and Reflection

The Christian life itself, when taken seriously, is a constant challenge to growth. Dr. Charles Elliot was conducting a series of Biblical Meditations. A lady who was attending came to him half-way through and said, "Your meditations have done nothing for me . . . until today when you told us to let the Lord speak directly to us. He has never spoken to me before, but today he did, and do you know what he said? 'For Pete's sake — grow up' . . . Now what do you think he meant by that?" (*Praying the Kingdom,* Darton, Longman and Todd).

The Christian life begins in baptism or conversion — according to your own theological understanding and your personal experience — but whenever it begins, in this life, it is never complete. It inspires an ongoing search for valid experience and convincing truth. It is not an easy pursuit and it always has peaks and troughs. Hopefully, however, as you look back over the months and years, you can discern some progress. In this search for growth and ever deepening experience we are in good company (see Philippians 3:14).

The knowledge that we are being cared for and encouraged in this process is a factor of enormous significance. Those who have been helped in a time of illness by a good doctor, will sometimes say, "It wasn't just his medical knowledge and skill. I felt that he really cared." Similarly with teachers. Those who really care for boys and girls as individuals will inspire them far more than those who, although highly qualified academically, are cold and clinical in their teaching. The latter kind may impart facts and information; it is those who care who inspire enthusiasm and vision.

So one of the aims of true Christian caring is to promote growth of personality and a developing Christian experience. Another way of putting it is to enable growth into 'wholeness' or 'holiness' (see Colossians 2:6-7). How do we play our part in this exciting adventure?

1. By helping people to understand themselves better.

This sounds presumptuous — as though we believe that we can do good to people! This reaction is modified when we recognise that we are all sharing in the same pilgrimage, and we all need help and support from one another. Humbly we believe that we may have insights to offer — but, at the same time, we acknowledge that we also need help from others. Caring is a mutual experience.

The raw material for better self-understanding lies in examining the kind of things we say to ourselves and in paying careful attention to our feelings. I recall once being at a meeting where a certain report was being discussed. I had gone with some carefully prepared comments but, so intense was the debate, that I had difficulty in gaining a hearing. Eventually, when I was called on to speak, I felt that not much notice was being taken of my contribution. I felt hurt. My reactions were childish of course and, later on that evening, when I was going over the events in my mind, I recognised this and offered my negative feelings to God in a time of quiet. I now listened more carefully to my 'inner voice' and recognised how negative and indeed, destructive, my feelings had been.

There was an interesting sequel to this happening. The person who had been mainly responsible for preparing the report in question had felt threatened by the whole proceedings. Sometime later I was able to share with her my own response to her report and how hurt I had originally felt because little notice was taken of my views. She responded positively to me, but also felt free to express the disappointment and anger she had felt on that day. This had clouded her judgement and prevented her from seeing that the people who had been critical were genuinely wanting to improve the work that she had done. They valued the substance of the report but wanted changes in the details. Eventually the whole matter came to a satisfactory conclusion, but the turning point for her was when we were both willing to express our vulnerability to one another.

So, if we can help others to discern the true nature of their feelings by listening to what they are saying to themselves via the 'inner voice', we shall have done them a real service. Here are just a few of the things people say to themselves, often as the result of a specific happening:

> I must be seen to be successful.
> I must not displease others by making mistakes.
> I want to be loved and appreciated.
> I shall feel better if things work out exactly as I want them to.

When things do not go well we tend to . . .

> Be angry with ourselves.
> Be resentful and dislike the people we think are responsible.

Through the recognition of this process comes developing self-awareness which promotes growth and maturity. This is much more likely to happen when we are being helped by someone who cares enough for us to take the risk of being honest and open with us. When things like this have happened to us, we become more confident and able to facilitate similar things happening to other people.

One positive sign of progress is when people are able to laugh at themselves. I can recall saying to myself on numerous occasions: "Hello, hello, here we go again — I'm up to my old tricks!" The ability to do this is a genuine gift from God.

So if we are helping other people to grow we are sharing in God's plans for their development. They are his children and he desires that they should find greater fulfilment and purpose in their lives. How does the Bible help us along this particular way?

a) See Proverbs 23:7 in the Authorised Version. This verse underlines the importance of our thought lives.

b) Compare Psalm 139:23-24 and Hebrews 4:12. The person who faces the challenge outlined here must be highly motivated.

c) See Mark 7:14–23. Actions originate in thoughts. How can we reach the heights of 2 Corinthians 10:5 and Philippians 4:6-9, 11 and 13?

d) See Ephesians 4:22-25. How does 'speaking the truth' improve the relationships we have with people? Do we ever have to be 'economical with the truth' in the best interests of the person we are trying to help?

2. By helping people to discover and develop their potential through facing up constructively to challenge.

Life does not run always on an even keel. Challenges, frustration, fears, anxiety, sadness and loss. These are experiences we all face sooner or later.

A dear friend died when she was at the height of her powers and usefulness. The members of the Church to which she belonged had been praying earnestly for her and she died triumphantly and in peace, but many in the Church wondered why such persistent prayer had not brought about her physical restoration. Her minister in a sermon preached immediately after her passing, suggested that at this stage questions beginning with *what* rather than with *why* were the best questions to ask. Not "Why has this happened?" but "What is the Lord saying to us as a Church through this sad event?" Many said afterwards that their Church had been strengthened by this happening.

Similarly in a very different set of circumstances I know a man who now is grateful for being made redundant. That event pushed him into starting his own business which he had wanted to do for years but, up till then, he had lacked the courage.

Yet again, I know several people who have actually been pleased (afterwards) that they became seriously ill. The event had caused them to re-assess their lives, examine their priorities — and adopt a different life-style.

The caring which enables development and growth in these and related situations must be sensitive and understanding, since it can so easily be misunderstood. Those of us who are parents know that there were times in our relationships with our children that it was essential that we did not take over and so prevent them facing up to their own challenges. It hurt us when we saw them making mistakes, but we recognised that this was part of the process of growing up. At that stage our love was best shown by their knowing that their parents were a backstop to whom they could turn for help and support when they asked for it.

So our friends and acquaintances often need a listening ear and a sounding board to bounce their thoughts and concerns against, when they are passing through a difficult period or a time of special challenge. They do not want instant solutions, nor to be treated to the 'if I were you' syndrome; they just want someone to share their dilemmas with and sometimes, to help them to sort out the various scenarios of possible response.

To stand with someone in times of stress and strain

can be a means of growth, both for those who care and for those who are being cared for.

a) Read 2 Samuel 12:1-15. Look for courage, conviction, rationalisation, penitence etc. Was David a better man because he had sinned?

b) Read Isaiah 6:1-8. How would you say Isaiah grew up as a result of what happened to him in the Temple?

c) What happened to Paul in the events he describes in 2 Corinthians 12:1-10? Can you identify with him?

Suggestions for Group Activity

1. Go round the group inviting brief comments on the points made, with their Biblical references, at the end of each of the two sections in the study and reflection material supplied. As in the previous week do not invite discussion of each point at this stage. Use this process to get everyone involved.

2. Invite anyone from the group who has been trained through The Samaritans, a Citizen's Advice Bureau or within a counselling agency, to tell how this training made a difference (if it did) to the way they functioned as persons.

3. Invite sharing from group members as to how they felt they dealt with the different challenges they have received. Did they feel that they *grew* through the experience? What kind of help did they receive during those times? Did any well intentioned people try to help them but only make matters worse? If so — why and in what way?

4. Summarise the implications of some of the Bible verses and feed them into the Meditation.

Example: Lord, you have bidden us to bring every thought in captivity to Christ and to fill our minds with the things that are good and worthy of praise. Show to us how this is possible, for our thoughts often wander and our minds get filled with longings of which we feel deeply ashamed. (2 Corinthians 10:5 and Philippians 4:6-9).

Suggestions for a Closing Meditation

"... but to listen, to listen intently, my God I wish I could listen to my brother, listen to his heart beats, listen to those faint, O so faint . . . calls which are there hidden under, I know not what, some sort of fear . . ." (Jean Vanier in *Tears of Silence,* Darton, Longman and Todd.)

FRIENDS OF JESUS

"You are my friends if you do what I command you . . . You did not choose me but I chose you and appointed you that you should go and bear fruit and that your fruit should abide" (John 15: 15-16).

THE PRIVILEGE OF FRIENDSHIP

Friends delight in each other's company. Use your imagination to visualise Jesus in the midst. Marvel that you can be his friend. Rejoice because you know that his friendship is for ever and he is always available.

Chorus: "Jesus we adore you"

THE RESPONSIBILITIES OF FRIENDSHIP

To love is to encourage, to value,
to give strength,
to accept the other as he is.
Love is not asking: what can you give me?
but: What can I give you?
(J. de Rooy in *Tools for Meditation,* The Grail)

Chorus: "Jesus we adore you"

THE GROUPS OFFER THEIR PRAYERS BASED ON SCRIPTURE VERSES

TIME IS SPENT IN SILENCE AS WE THINK MORE ABOUT HOW WE CAN HELP OTHERS TO GROW THROUGH THE WAYS IN WHICH WE CARE FOR THEM.

THE LAST WORD:

"True listening . . . means our moving away from the centre of attention and inviting others into that space . . . From experience we know how healing such an invitation can be. When someone listens to us with deep concentration and expresses sincere care for our struggles and pains, we feel that something very deep is happening to us. Slowly fears melt away, tensions dissolve, anxieties retreat, and we discover that we carry something within us, something we can trust and offer as a gift to others" (From *Compassion* by Nouwen, McNeill and Morrison; Darton, Longman and Todd.)

Topical Introduction

The first suggestion is that you use a selection of the pastoral situations provided at the beginning of this course. They could be read or, better still, you could "role-play" them. You will see that they are all open-ended.

The role-plays could, however, be taken a stage further by the person who is trying to help saying all the *wrong* things and making all the *wrong* kind of responses. Those planning this could make use of the following sentences:

"Oh, I'm sure it's not as bad as all that."

"If I were you this is exactly what I would do."

"It's bound to turn out right in the end."

"I'm sorry but I don't see how any Christian could behave like this. There's nothing I can do to help you."

"I've had a very similar experience; let me tell you all about it."

"Cheer up, think of all the good times you had together."

"Let's pray about it; God will give us the answer."

Yet another way of using the role plays would be to deal with two or three of the situations and have them played . . .

a) The wrong way — using some of the above sentences.

b) The right way — in the light of the study and reflection material.

The contrast would then be vivid in the minds of the course members.

Material for Study and Reflection

A crisis occurs in someone's life through a traumatic event which evokes deep feelings. There are many different kinds of crises — serious illness, bereavement, losing a job, marital failure, alcohol and gambling problems, guilt feelings following upon some social failure, religious doubt after many years of stable faith, suicidal tendencies. The list is endless. We all come face to face with such events at some time, either in our own lives or in the lives of people close to us.

The first thing to say about caring for others in crises is that it is a demanding exercise which will call upon all the resources we possess, spiritual, mental, emotional — and, indeed, physical. There is much that can be discovered about caring for people in stress situations, through experiences others make available in books and on courses like this one.

There are techniques which come mainly from the disciplines of psychotherapy and counselling. These can help us but the most important factor is the kind of people we are. Caring is more than a good habit which can be learnt; it is an expression of the true nature of our own beings, refined through our own experiences and those which others have made available to us.

The Biblical basis for our caring lies in the two-fold command to love God and to love our neighbour (Matthew 22:34-40; Mark 12: 28-34; Luke 10: 25-28). We are also told quite explicitly to love our enemies (Matthew 5: 43-47 and Luke 6: 27-36).

Loving our neighbour, and so caring for him or her, is a direct consequence of our own discovering that we are loved by God. Caring in crises (or at any other time), is, ideally, the free flow of our own gratitude to God, being directed towards another person's need. Just as it is true that we have the ability to love because God first loved us (1 John 4:19), so it is also true that we can only serve and care if and when we are aware that God serves and cares and that this was made explicit in Jesus (Philippians 2: 5-7).

The fact that in Luke's gospel the command to love is immediately followed by thc Parable of the Good Samaritan (Luke 10: 28-37), adds an important point. True Christian love issues in direct action.

John's Gospel underlines this point by the very actions of Jesus himself. It was indeed a crisis point in his own ministry when he met with the disciples in the Upper Room. It was crisis time for Judas — and he failed. Jesus then brought the momentous events of that evening to a dramatic conclusion by washing his disciple's feet. Then he said to them: "Now you know this truth, how happy you will be if you put it into practice" (John 13:17).

Share ourselves

The first step is always to make ourselves available to people in need; to provide space for them. We may not as yet have many pastoral caring skills, although the fact that we are sharing in this course indicates our desire to become better at this task; but first people must feel that we do care for them and that our care is authentic and genuine. This creates the empathy which is vital in any caring relationship.

Make use of other people's experience

As we have already seen, we do not care effectively with a text-book in our hands or even with a set of guide-lines imprinted upon our minds. Given our integrity and sincerity, however, there are many useful insights we can discover, and, equally important, we may be saved from making mistakes.

Listen and attend

To listen and attend is priority number one. The person in need requires our whole attention and the quality of the relationship which we establish will depend upon their feeling that we are listening to them with the whole of our being. This will only happen if we *really are listening*. The discipline of schooling ourselves to *hear* what they are saying and then try to enter into their feelings is sometimes difficult. We so easily tend to jump to conclusions and offer instant solutions.

Don't give immediate advice

This is the quickest way to destroy a caring relationship. Sometimes the answer to another person's problem seems perfectly obvious to someone who is not emotionally involved. At all costs avoid saying, "If I were you I would . . . " When a person does seek your actual advice give it only tentatively, "I wonder if you have ever considered the possibility of . . . "

Be realistic in your attempts at reassurance

Sometimes would-be carers think that they are being helpful by insisting that it will all be well in the end: "The doctor will take care of it", or "She is bound to come back when she realises what she is missing." Neither of these things may actually happen, and, in any case, the person in need is aware that you cannot really know. Being and remaining with them may well be the most important aspect of caring in the early stages of a crisis.

Don't be judgemental

The revelations emerging from a trusting relationship may be so horrifying that we are tempted to jump in with, "how could you possibly do such a thing!" However shocked we may feel, it will do little good to dispense instant condemnation. This does not mean that we ignore our own ethical and moral standards, nor that we believe that Christian love eliminates our proper sense of justice. The person most concerned will no doubt be acutely aware of his or her failure. It is their own judgement upon themselves which will eventually lead to penitence and, in some cases, reparation. When all such events are being discussed, we need to be gentle and understanding.

We have splendid examples of this in our Lord's teaching on the judgement of others in Matthew 7: 1-6, and in his attitude towards the woman taken in adultery in John 8:1-11.

Use open-ended questions and reflect back your awareness

Questions should be used sparingly in crisis situations. When they are used, they should assist the person in need to tell their own story and particularly to express their feelings. Questions like, "How long have you been married?" require only factual answers. Questions like, "How have you been feeling since you were left on your own?" enable the person concerned to open up more of themselves.

What often does move a situation along helpfully is to try to reflect back what you sense the person is feeling: "I hear you saying that your negative feelings about your husband go back to the time of your illness". In some books on pastoral care this process is called 'mirroring'.

Don't let your problems take over

The shared vulnerability of two people can be helpful, as we have already seen, but we must beware of shutting off the expression of their needs by a long and detailed description of our own. An indication that your own experiences help your understanding of the problem may be useful, but don't overdo it! In this crisis-encounter, it is the other person who comes first.

Help the other person to move towards some course of action

Crisis situations can be so overwhelming that the person concerned is paralysed. They feel totally incapable of any action. The events are dictating the course of what happens and they are not influencing, in any way, the pattern of those events. Slowly your task is to help them to make positive moves. If it is a sudden death, then there are practical matters to be dealt with such as the funeral. If it is a desertion, then legal advice may be necessary. If it is a moral failure, the consequences have to be faced and a new beginning made.

The whole process may take a very long time but, providing the one you are helping is moving forward in a positive way, time doesn't matter. Indeed, the longer the time taken, the more positive and lasting may be the end results. Actions initiated too quickly may be regretted afterwards.

Be aware that God can use crises

In our previous week's study (Caring for Growth), we saw that God can use crisis situations. Prayerfully we need to be saying to ourselves, "What is hidden in this situation which, when revealed, may open up new depths of personality and enhanced spirituality?" Healing and renewal do come from facing realistically the darker side of our personalities, including our sins and failures.

Consider the place of prayer

This should arise naturally and always be related to the situation facing the person we are trying to help. If the person is unfamiliar with the practice of prayer then to suggest it openly may embarrass them and so prove unhelpful. However, if a good relationship has been established and the needy person knows of your own Christian commitment then, at the opportune time, the suggestion can be made. The right to do this should not be taken for granted but a simple question like: "Would you like us to put this whole matter before God in prayer?" may evoke a positive response — but not always.

If and when we pray, we do not ask God for instantaneous solutions; we simply put the issues trustingly in His hands. The use of helpful scripture quotations can be part of a meditative kind of prayer. Allow for long pauses. In the creative silence God will often bring calm and release. Where appropriate, lay hands upon them in blessing and assure them they are surrounded by God's love. Use 2 Corinthians 12: 7-10.

The crisis of bereavement

A lot of work has been attempted with bereaved people in recent years. This has brought to light a series of reactions which seem to occur frequently in those who have lost a loved one. They do not all appear in every case and they do not always follow in the same sequence. It is useful however, to be aware of what may happen in bereavement situations, and it is also true that some other situations (desertion, unexpected redundancy) are very much akin to bereavement. Consequently, similar reactions may occur.

The various stages are picked out in many books. I summarise here what they say:

Shock — inability to accept what has happened; acting in a 'wooden-like' manner; being dazed.

Release —tears; hysteria. People find release in different ways. I recall visiting a man years ago whose wife had just been killed in an accident. He was digging his garden; his way of finding release.

Depression — usually after the funeral when the 'tumult and the shouting' has died down. Depressive bouts following upon bereavement can last for a long time and call for a lot of understanding friendship and personal support.

Guilt — "What should I have done which I didn't do?" "I could have been a better wife/husband etc."

Anger — God is the object of much anger because "He allowed it to happen". Clergy and church folk generally may be thought of as "God's representatives" and so the anger is sometimes focussed on them.

Preoccupation with the loss — this can come in a variety of ways such as sleeping with a photograph of the deceased; keeping their clothes ready for use. Only when such behaviour is prolonged and becomes obsessive is it not a part of natural grieving.

Resolution — this takes longer with some than with others, but eventually new life patterns develop and reality is accepted. There are swings of moods but usually the progress is in an upward direction.

Suggestions for Group Activity

1. Ask *well in advance* if there are two or three members of the group who are willing to share a real life experience in which they faced a crisis. Ask them to describe the kind of help they received at the time. What aspects of that help were positive and what aspects were negative? Perhaps some group member might feel able to describe how they feel that they failed someone in a crisis situation.

2. Look at the story of "The Woman at the Well" in John 4: 5-30. Is the way Jesus related to her a pattern of pastoral caring for us?

   Look out for . . . .

   The way the relationship was established
   The open ended questions
   The promise of help
   The opening up of the real problem
   The uncovering of the truth without direct condemnation
   The consequences of the meeting

3. Do the varying stages of bereavement described in this study ring true for group members? Have you observed them in others? Do we take the pastoral care of the bereaved seriously enough? Could we do more as churches?

Suggestions for a Closing Meditation

"I recall with immense gratitude a man who greatly helped me through my own teenage traumas. He was about twenty years older than myself but was near enough to the kind of experiences through which I was passing to be sensitive to them when he saw them being acted out in my own life. He did not preach at me (although he was a professional preacher); he did not attempt to 'mould' me in any particular direction. Instead he provided me with an opportunity to share with him some of my fears, hopes and anticipations. He listened with evident interest and genuine understanding" (The author in *Stepping Stones to Christian Maturity — Bible Reading Fellowship)*.

READ MARK 2: 1-12

REFLECT IN SILENCE AFTER EACH OF THE FOLLOWING POINTS:

The paralysed man had friends who put him directly in the presence of Jesus.

Jesus discerned his total needs. They were both physical and spiritual.

The paralysed man had to play his part. He obeyed the command of Jesus to pick up his pallet and walk.

The assembled people praised God.

WE RESOLVE TO BRING OUR FRIENDS INTO THE PRESENCE OF JESUS BY . . .

Providing a listening ear.
Paying attention to the needs of those around us.
Stretching out our hands in love and friendship.
Developing our pastoral caring role.

SING THE HYMN WRITTEN BY THE REV. F. PRATT GREEN —

O Christ the healer, we have come,
To pray for health, to plead for friends.

THE LAST WORD: "Let us not grow weary in well-doing, for in due course we shall reap, if we do not lose heart. So then, as we have opportunity, let us do good to all" (Galatians 6: 9-10).

Topical Introduction

Prepare a tape-recording in which different voices share certain imaginary experiences. They are imaginary only in the sense that they are actual experiences which have not actually happened to the people who are telling the story. In fact similar happenings have taken place many, many times. The intention is to highlight how people feel when adequate and understanding care is not offered. The material provided could be easily expanded.

1. I am physically handicapped. In appearance I could be described as grotesque and I often make unusual sounds. My mind however, is in good working order and I know what my condition is. There are many things I find difficult. Eating for instance, is a problem and I know that my way of eating is distasteful to some people. So I tend to want to eat only with people more like myself or alone. This hurts me because I long to make happy relationships with all kinds of people. I have often felt rejected and it doesn't help when people who think they are being kind, treat me like a small child and want to feed me with a spoon.

2. I am dying. I am fully aware of the fact that I have only a few weeks to live. The doctor in charge of my case seldom comes to see me now. He sends his junior who seems afraid of me and never looks me in the eye. Also I have been put into a small room on my own with no one to talk to except when members of my family come. I have not been consulted about the drugs I am being given and strongly suspect that they are to keep me asleep for most of the time.

3. I have a serious illness. I know this because of my growing incapacity. I have seen a number of doctors who have given me some information, but not enough. The senior doctor in charge of my case told me to put myself in his hands and he would do his best for me. He spoke kindly but did not want to go into any details. I told him that I wanted to be involved in the treatment process and that, in fact, there were certain things I thought I could do

to help myself. He smiled benignly and said, "Best leave it to the experts". I asked the hospital chaplain about my illness but his reply was, "Nobody tells me anything — I'm supposed just to look after your soul".

Material for Study and Reflection

An American doctor, Eric J. Cassell, wrote a book in the mid-seventies entitled *The Healer's Art* (published in the UK by Penguin). While maintaining his faith in the most up-to-date scientific methods of medical diagnosis and treatment, he suggests that modern technological developments need to be accompanied by an exploration into the powerful effects of human relationships in the treatment of sick people. He believes that two doctors who both utilise the most sophisticated methods of diagnosis and treatment, but who differ markedly in the way they each relate to their patients, will, over a period of time, see widely differing results. Both will be instrumental in curing patients from their illness symptoms; the one who cares to the point where he or she is prepared to get involved in the patient's life, thoughts, fears and anxieties, may bring healing as well as cure.

He believes also that scientific detachment in the treatment of patients does not produce happy and fulfilled doctors. His own method of combining a rigorous, scientific approach with a willingness to become involved in the patients' inner lives, gives him profound satisfaction. He attempts to practice the *art* as well as the *science* of medicine. In other words — *caring does heal*.

Care of the disabled

In recent years much thought has been given to the pastoral care of the disabled and, in 1987, a new movement was launched entitled Church Action on Disability (CHAD). The movement is concerned with better facilities for disabled people (ramps, lifts, loop systems, improved toilets, wider use of sign language etc.), but such improvements, while important, are not CHAD's main concern. The primary aim is to change attitudes.

'Acceptance' is a word that trips easily from the tongue: "Of course we accept handicapped people

— don't we organise a special party for them every Christmas? Don't we support all their flag days and street collections and indeed organise some of them on their behalf?" If we really examine ourselves, however, we know that this does not represent 'acceptance' at all. It indicates a paternalistic (and sometimes patronising) attitude towards the handicapped. Much more careful thought and self-examination is required before so-called 'normal' people people act in a truly caring way towards the handicapped.

A good way to begin is by recognising and acknowledging the fears within us. Some forms of handicap are disturbing: the jerky movements of the spastic; the fits and contortions of the epileptic; the appearance and speech limitations of those with Down's Syndrome. But people who have these limitations are still people. The problem so often lies within ourselves. Once good human relationships are established, fears quickly disappear.

One way of deepening our relationships with handicapped people is to recognise that we are all disabled in one way or another. Some handicaps may be less obvious than others, but they are just as real. Neurotic fear and anxiety can be crippling disabilities but many people cope with them and, by wearing a mask, are socially acceptable. Those who are slaves to habits (excessive eating, drinking, smoking) are also disabled people. A more open acknowledgement of our own handicaps, both to ourselves as well as to others, would create a more wholesome atmosphere and would improve our relationships with those whose handicaps are more immediately obvious.

So, because we are all handicapped in one way or another we belong to a mutual society. The handicapped are not our weaker brothers and sisters — they are part of God's family — and they are our equals. They have a contribution to make to the worship, fellowship and service of the local church. They must be on the giving as well as the receiving end. Whatever be the nature of our handicap we all need each other. This kind of deep and meaningful fellowship will demonstrate that *caring does heal*.

Look to Jesus

We began this course by thinking about 'Jesus who cares'. Now, in this our final study, we need to look at him again so that we might be vividly conscious of his example. Again and again in his earthly ministry he showed that *caring does heal*.

Before Jesus healed anyone he felt deeply for their needs. In Matthew 9:36 we read of his deep concern for the physical, mental and spiritual needs of those who flocked to him. Is there a difference between pity and compassion?

In Matthew 15:22-39 he had healed many people but still felt for their needs and so took appropriate action. Are there implications here for the wide range of caring which is required of us?

Look at some of the individuals Jesus cared for and helped: a leper (Mark 1:41); the woman with an alabaster box of ointment (Luke 7:47 is the key verse); two blind men (Matthew 20:34). Who could they represent today: a person with Aids; a prostitute; the spiritually blind?

Jesus did not only cure; he called for a total response of trust and obedience (see Mark 2: 1-12 and John 5:14).

What do you think the attitude of Jesus did for Zacchaeus (Luke 19:9-10)? Recall the reference to the Woman at the Well in a previous study. What kind of relationship was established with her? (John 4:29)?

Such examples surely require the followers of Jesus today to "go and do likewise". This is made explicit by Paul who lays out an operational plan for God's people (Colossians 3:12-17), and this is underlined by Peter (1 Peter 3:8-17).

So again and again Jesus showed how a caring attitude encourages healing and promotes wholeness.

Caring liberates our powers of self-healing

As most doctors and therapists readily acknowledge, they do not themselves bring healing. However through surgery, drugs, psychotherapy, good advice and a patient's change in life-style, 'blockages' can be removed or neutralised, and then the natural, God-given, healing powers can get to work.

A powerful addition to good medical care is found when sick people become aware that they are surrounded by love and care: "Do not be afraid for I have redeemed you; I have called you by your name, you are mine . . ." (Isaiah 43:1). As we have already been reminded, God's love is frequently mediated by human love. When a loving and caring person brings home to us the truth that we are loved by them, and through them by none other than God himself, regenerative powers are released within us.

Canon Frank Wright points out in *The Pastoral Nature of Healing* (SCM Press) that 'Mothering' or 'Good Parenting' is a vital factor in the healing process. He quotes the late Dr. Bob Lambourne as saying that as high as 70% of medical care and treatment of minor ailments is carried out by mothers, relatives and neighbours. And even when caring is carried out by professionals, the 'mothering' element is of vital importance.

Thirty years as a hospital chaplain has brought me into touch with many doctors and with many more patients. Those doctors who have been appreciated most have been those who have established open and trusting relationships with their patients, and have tried to understand their feelings. Those who have been coldly clinical in their approach may have been efficient, but they have not been so successful in securing the patient's active co-operation by which natural healing forces have been released.

Enquiring minds naturally ask how prayer for sick people can promote their healing. One answer is that those who know that they are being prayed for, and that their friends are spending time in prayer concentrating upon their needs, begin to feel better because of the human solidarity which is being shown. This in itself is a powerful therapy. Sincere prayer forms a link between a person's need and God's rich grace.

Similarly the 'laying on of hands' is a sign and symbol of God's love combined with real human concern. That is why I feel that this ministry should be personal to the one who seeks this blessing as a 'means of grace'. This can be conveyed through the warmth of a sensitive and loving touch and by the intimacy of the accompanying prayer. That such a ministry should be the focal point of continuing pastoral care is also important. God uses the channels of caring compassion and sincere human concern to convey his healing grace.

I am not suggesting that this is all that is happening when we pray for people and minister to them by the 'laying on of hands'. The ways in which God meets human need defy definition and are beyond our understanding, but sincere human care reflects God's care and, as such, is a vital factor in the healing process.

Caring provides strength in suffering

Dr. Frances Young wrote in The Methodist Recorder (18.2.88) about a week-end conference she was leading attended by people she knew well. She had taken with her Arthur, her handicapped son and she and her husband had just been told by a doctor that there was nothing more which could be done for Arthur's physical twistedness. Arthur was only able to share in the music, but as they studied sin and suffering he was there as a reminder that "bad things do happen to good people". At breakfast on the last day a lady present who had a handicapped grandchild said: "You know this week-end has changed my attitude. I kept praying desperately for a miracle, but now I see that there may be a better way." That better way, Frances testified, is the way of love that never fails.

We must never allow ourselves to have too narrow a concept of healing and to think of it mainly in relation to the physical changes and improvements we quite naturally long to see. When we put people in God's hands (including ourselves) we have every right to ask for their healing; for their growing wholeness; but we must never demand that healing shall come in a particular way. Whatever way it comes — and come it will — we give thanks to God who cares. Caring does promote healing, sometimes of the mind and spirit that we may triumph over bodily weakness. Bonhoeffer was not ashamed to reveal his fears and his anxiety in his wonderful poem *Who am I?* but he ended in quiet confidence:

> *Who am I? They mock me these lonely questions of mine.*
> *Whoever I am, Thou knowest O God, I am thine.*

Caring brings healing at the end

A modern hospice presents a powerful model of the way God uses human care to bring peace at the end. There are certain distinctive features of hospice life which could and should enlighten the general hospital and domestic scene.

Care in a hospice provides the maximum comfort within weakness and disease. The medical needs of the patient are given a high priority and pain and nausea are carefully controlled.

Care in a hospice is offered on an honest and open basis which eschews lies and deceit. When patients ask for information they are told the truth. Those who have shared the hospice experience, either as relatives of patients, staff, or the patients themselves, speak warmly of the atmosphere which prevails in which love and togetherness flourish.

Care in a hospice is shot through and through with hope. A quiet but infectious faith lies at the heart of the whole operation. Of course there is no religious pressure. Patients are encouraged to relax in God's love and be at peace.

The Dean of Salisbury told some friends how disturbed he was, in the early stages of his parish ministry, when some on whom he had laid hands for healing died immediately afterwards. He spoke to a trusted spiritual adviser who suggested that perhaps he had actually given them permission to die and had helped them to discover their final healing in Christ.

Caring does heal. We all need both to give and receive care because as children of the light we possess only a little light. Our light cannot grow unless we share it with another. As we care so do we . . . "bear each other's burdens and so fulfil the law of Christ".

Suggestions for Group Activity

1. Go through the Bible references and ask what were the practical things which flowed from the compassion which Jesus showed. Make a list of them. Do they move you to think of any caring activity you had not thought of previously? Share your thoughts.

2. How many handicapped people do we know who play a full part in the life of their local Church? Does it flow from this that something should be done locally about CHAD, Church Action on Disability? (You could write for more information to CHAD, Charisma Cottage, Drewsteignton, Exeter, EX6 6QR.)

3. Have you any experiences to share of how caring released a person's self-healing powers?

4. "To be drugged into dying is to miss a real slice of life". How do you react to that statement?

Suggestions for a Closing Meditation

"By the honest recognition of our human sameness, we can participate in the care of God who came, not to the powerful, but to the powerless, not to be different, but the same, not to take our pain away, but to share it. Through this participation we can open our hearts to one another and form a new community."

(Henri Nouwen *Out of Solitude* Ave Maria Press)

GOD CARES

"Casting all your care upon him; for he careth for you." (1 Peter 5:7).

"Cast your burden upon the Lord, and he will sustain you." (Psalm 55:22).

JESUS CARED

"And when he was come near, he beheld the city, and wept over it." (Luke 19:41).

"I will pray the Father, and he shall give you another Comforter, that he may abide with you for ever. Even the Spirit of truth." (John 14:16-17).

CARING DOES HEAL

"This then is love's demand — not merely to be skilled in discerning and reflecting the feelings of others — but to be present to them in such an open and peaceful way that our love and God's love seem one and the same . . . Most of our meetings with others may appear quite superficial and ineffective. But just occasionally we are the ones to mediate love's power."

Paid to Care (Alastair Campbell, SPCK)

THINK PRAYERFULLY ABOUT —

Someone who is handicapped.
Someone who is dying.
Someone who is ill.

OFFER TO GOD THE WAY YOU ARE GOING TO SEEK TO BRING HEALING TO THEM THROUGH YOUR CARING.

THE LAST WORD —

"Jesus, Risen Lord,
you change and transfigure our heart just as it is,
You do not even ask us to uproot the weeds;
you take care of that.
With our own wounds, the thorns that hurt us,
you light a fire — and a way forward opens in us
to welcome your Spirit of compassion and the Spirit
of praise that brings healing."

(Brother Roger of Taizé)

Bibliography and References

Booth, Howard, *Stepping Stones to Christian Maturity,* Bible Reading Fellowship.

Bryant, Christopher, *Jung and the Christian Faith,* Darton, Longman and Todd.

Campbell, Alastair, *Paid to Care,* SPCK.

Cassell, Eric J., *The Healer's Art,* Penguin.

Clinebell, Howard, *Mental Health through Christian Community,* Abingdon Press.

Collins, Gary, *Innovative Approaches to Counselling,* Word Books.

Dale, Alan, *New World,* Oxford University Press.

Dale, Alan, *Winding Quest,* Oxford University Press.

Elliott, Charles, *Praying the Kingdom,* Darton, Longman and Todd.

Manson, T. W., *On Paul and John.* Quoted in the Preface to *New World,* OUP.

Mary Clare, Mother, *Encountering the Depths,* Darton, Longman and Todd.

Nouwen, Henri, *Out of Solitude,* Ave Maria Press.

Nouwen, McNeill and Morrison, *Compassion,* Darton, Longman and Todd.

Pietroni, Patrick, *Holistic Living,* Dent.

Ramon, Brother, *Life's Changing Seasons,* Marshall Pickering.

Rooy, J. de, *Tools for Meditation,* The Grail.

Sanford, John, *Ministry Burnout,* Arthur James.

Stewart, James, *The Life and Teaching of Jesus Christ,* Saint Andrew Press.

Tugwell, Simon, *Ways of Imperfection,* Darton, Longman and Todd.

Wright, Frank. *The Pastoral Nature of Healing,* SCM Press.

Wright, H. Norman, *Self-Talk, Imagery and Prayer in Counselling,* Word Books.

Young, Frances, *Newspaper article on February 18, 1988,* in The Methodist Recorder.

ARTHUR JAMES
publishes

THE NEW TESTAMENT: a translation by WILLIAM BARCLAY
in hardback and paperback

and the following WILLIAM BARCLAY books

The Mind of Jesus
Crucified and Crowned
Through the Year with William Barclay
Every Day with William Barclay
Marching Orders
Marching On

Also available through Arthur James

Seven Fresh Wineskins
(expositions of Old Testament passages)

Arthur James Limited
One Cranbourne Road, London N10 2BT
Tel: 081 883 1831/2201 0386 446 566 Fax: 081 883 8307